MIDDLESBROUGH
THEN & NOW
IN COLOUR

PAUL MENZIES

The
History
Press

I would like to dedicate this book to Jackie, Bob Menzies,
the Kirtley's and the late Wilf Mannion.

Footballer Wilf Mannion, who represented Middlesbrough, England and Great Britain, is one of the town's most famous sons. Nicknamed the 'Golden Boy', Wilf was inducted into the English Football Hall of Fame in 2004. An unassuming man, I was proud to be able to call Wilf Mannion a friend. In dedicating this book to Wilf, I am fulfilling a promise I once made to him.

First published in 2012

The History Press
The Mill, Brimscombe Port
Stroud, Gloucestershire, GL5 2QG
www.thehistorypress.co.uk

© Paul Menzies, 2012

The right of Paul Menzies to be identified as the Author
of this work has been asserted in accordance with the
Copyrights, Designs and Patents Act 1988.

ISBN 978 0 7524 6181 6

Typesetting and origination by The History Press
Printed in India.

CONTENTS

ACKNOWLEDGEMENTS

I give grateful thanks to all those individuals and organisations that have allowed me to copy and use their material, given their time and generally helped in my research. I have taken a great deal of time in tracing and establishing ownership of all material and ensuring that permission for reproduction in this work has been given, whether in copyright or not.

Permission to include material, including images and written material, has been given by the late John Lindberg, Stockton-on Tees Borough Council Museums Service, Steve Wild at Stockton Reference Library, the now defunct Cleveland County Council Planning Department, Middlesbrough Reference Library, Janet Baker at Teesside Archives, Alan Sims at the *Evening Gazette* Teesside, Jeff and Vera Wilkinson, and Keith Kirtley. I would also like to thank Alan McKinnell for allowing me access to his material, and for his never-ending kindness and patience during the writing of this book. All other material is from my own collection.

Writing a book always impacts on those people closest to you and this is the case here. I would like to offer an enormous thank you to my wife Jackie, who has had to put up with many months of my rising at five o'clock in the morning to write before going off to work, as well as many rainy afternoons spent at either the Teesside Archives or Reference Library in Middlesbrough.

West Street, where it all began – the very first house built in the new town of Middlesbrough in 1831.

INTRODUCTION

This work is a pictorial comparison of Middlesbrough in the modern era with the town of the relatively recent past. Modern Middlesbrough doesn't have a history beyond the early nineteenth century, as it was essentially a child of the later stages of the Industrial Revolution. However, this is not to say that the town wasn't a key part of the industrial development of the region. Indeed, when development did come it was almost on an unprecedented scale, as green fields around Middlesbrough Farm rapidly transformed into a new town aptly referred to by William Gladstone on his visit in 1862 as 'an infant Hercules'.

It is an ironic conclusion that the loss of the rich Victorian heritage of Middlesbrough has almost been comparable to the pace of its original development. In the period since the end of the Second World War, particularly since 1960, a large number of the town's most important and impressive architectural artefacts have been swept away in a frenzy, which would almost suggest an urgent need to disassociate itself from the past. The list of lost buildings is indeed long; the Royal Exchange, schools, housing, almost all of the old town, Marton Hall, Gunnergate Hall – all have gone in my lifetime. Almost too late there has been a cessation of this on-going circus of demolition, and so some buildings remain as a physical reminder of the past and the proud history that represents so many past generations. For the rest, archive images will have to suffice.

At least we are fortunate enough to have a considerable photographic record of the history of Middlesbrough and it is now being given the attention it so richly deserves. No longer are archival treasures thrown away and, through the work of many local organisations and individuals, fragments of the past are being gathered to bring about an acknowledgement that Middlesbrough was a town which played a very important part in the development of industry, both locally and further afield. Looking at the old newspaper reports of events that took place in Middlesbrough over the past two centuries, the one thing that comes through time after time is the civic pride that was felt when recognition was given to the development of a community that had not even existed before 1830. These few images will, I hope, add to this and at least reveal something of the rich heritage of the town's past.

While I have attempted to ensure that there are no obvious mistakes in this work, I would like to apologise in advance for any errors that have been made, factual or otherwise. Please feel free to contact me if you know of any errors and I will update my records. In the same vein, if you have any further information regarding any aspect of Middlesbrough's history that you would like to share with me then please get in touch, especially if you have any images that you will allow me to copy. With computer technology they can be copied in minutes and, in the case of damaged material, they can even be restored to a state that is an improvement on the original print! Also, in digitally preserving these images, they are being saved in a form where they will not be destroyed or deteriorate.

Paul Menzies, 2012
m.menzies1@ntlworld.com

LINTHORPE ROAD:
THE MASHAM HOTEL

ONE OF THE town's best-known roads, Linthorpe Road, evolved from a country lane which ran
from the original town via old Linthorpe village to Stockton. A plan from 1845 shows the lane
ran through open countryside. The location of the present-day Hill Street Centre was occupied
by sites entitled 'Gardens' and the 'Old Brick Yard' with its adjacent large pond. These fields
stretched across to the river. The post-1850 rapid expansion of Victorian Middlesbrough south
beyond the original site saw the construction of densely packed rows of terraced housing,
as Linthorpe Road became established as a major route in the new development. This view,
close to the northern terminus of Linthorpe Road, shows the railway in the distance, with the

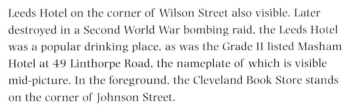

Leeds Hotel on the corner of Wilson Street also visible. Later destroyed in a Second World War bombing raid, the Leeds Hotel was a popular drinking place, as was the Grade II listed Masham Hotel at 49 Linthorpe Road, the nameplate of which is visible mid-picture. In the foreground, the Cleveland Book Store stands on the corner of Johnson Street.

ALTHOUGH SHOPPERS STILL throng to the retail outlets along Linthorpe Road, the mass demolition of local housing and subsequent depopulation of the town has seen its identity as a residential area largely changed. In particular, the closing of public houses means that an area once busy in the evening is now largely deserted. The Masham Hotel, one of the best known premises, closed as a hotel in the 1990s, becoming a retail outlet close to the entrance to the Hill Street Shopping Centre. Pedestrianisation means shoppers no longer have to do battle with traffic, but the hustle and bustle of former days remains a fond memory for many. If you look above the shop windows the original function of many of the buildings are still visible – a faded sign or a bricked-up window perhaps.

LINTHORPE ROAD:
THE CAFÉ ROYAL

THIS VIEW FROM 1911, with its crowded pavements of people gathering around the variety of shops, is taken further south down Linthorpe Road, close to the junction with Grange Road. An early Woolworth's store stands on the corner of Davison Street; this branch was the first in the North East and only the eighth in the country when it opened on 10 June 1911 at 91-93

Linthorpe Road. Across the road is Red Cross House (a chemist) while beyond that is the Café Royal, a popular meeting place for people before the First World War. To the right is Norton Street, one of many streets of terraced houses in the town centre that were hidden behind the bright façades of the shops.

THIS PHOTO WAS taken at the same location as the previous one – a glimpse of the first floor of Woolworths store can be seen. Today, the pedestrianised Linthorpe Road is still at the heart of Middlesbrough's retail world, though the buildings on the right have all long gone, replaced by The Cleveland Centre, a vibrant twenty-first-century shopping centre. There is a lot of debate whether these modern shopping complexes lack character, but they are considered by many to be 'of their time', providing shopping facilities in an ultra-modern environment.

LINTHORPE ROAD AND BOROUGH ROAD

IN THIS VIEW from 1930, a tram, complete with advert for Binns, trundles along Linthorpe Road close to the junction with Borough Road. Shoppers crowd the pavements passing the Elite Cinema (as it was then known) on the left. The Elite attracted huge audiences during the heyday of cinema in the 1930s – note that three daily shows are advertised, including an afternoon matinee at 2.30 p.m. The Elite opened in 1923, having replaced the Immanuel Baptist Church,

which itself could seat 300 people and was constructed at a cost of £2,300. The first service was held on 3 June 1888. Across the road is the Linthorpe Road Methodist Church, which opened on 28 August 1892, having been built on the site of an allotment garden – one of several in the town at that time.

THERE ARE A remarkable number of similarities between the old view and the modern one, taken almost eighty years later. In particular, the exterior of the old cinema building is still virtually unchanged, although it is now no longer a cinema, having been renamed the ABC in 1964 and then later closed as a cinema altogether. The elegant Edwardian properties on the right appear, at first glance, to be unchanged. The tramlines are gone but this is still a bus route, while the Linthorpe Road Methodist Church building is still there but no longer functions as a church. It is in the far distance that the most dramatic changes have occurred, with many buildings in and close to Linthorpe Road having been demolished to make way for the Cleveland Centre.

ALBERT ROAD

THIS NOSTALGIC IMAGE recalls life in Middlesbrough before the First World War, as the No. 51 tram travels along Albert Road. The horse-drawn vehicles and the men standing outside the Royal Exchange all portray another age. The tram is travelling along one of the main routes, from Linthorpe village to the terminus at Ferry Road in the old town. This service had to be a single decker to enable it to pass under the Albert Railway Bridge. Passengers looking out of the

window almost have time to look at the displays as they pass Newhouse's drapery store, where the white awnings provide shade for the front of the shop.

THE TRAM'S MODERN counterpart, an Arriva single deck bus, travels down Albert Road en route for the Town Hall. The financial and service businesses that occupied this stretch of Albert Road for many years have now either closed or relocated; as a result, many buildings have undergone a change of use, with several redeveloped or, as in the case of the Middlesbrough Exchange, demolished to make way for the A66. One structure that has survived is the Albert Railway Bridge, just visible beyond the A66 road bridge.

CORPORATION ROAD

TAKEN IN CORPORATION Road outside Burtons shop, which stood on the site of Collingwood's the jewellers, this wonderful period view from the early 1930s shows Saltmers and Wilsons on the left, with the buildings from the Wesley Chapel down to the Corporation Hotel on the right. As the hands on the Town Hall clock approach 4.30 p.m., two trams pass each other near the Empire Palace of Varieties, while a crowd of people have gathered close to the 'Wesley Hall' nameplate. Other people spill out onto the road, with seemingly little concern for any danger from passing traffic.

THE CONTEMPORARY VIEW (above) shows both old and new features of Middlesbrough. On the left it is still possible to locate buildings that are found in the previous image, with the wall of the former Wilson's building, on the corner of Dundas Street, still visible, and several properties in this row with relatively unchanged exteriors, although their retail usage is different. Opposite, however, modern structures – the Cleveland Centre and the giant CNE building – dominate the scene. In fact, you have to look very hard to see any part of the Town Hall – a building that dominates the previous image. The pedestrianisation of Corporation Road is another change. It is pleasing to note that the terracotta bricks of the Empire Theatre are still visible in the distance.

EXCHANGE PLACE
AND WILSON STREET

HENRY BOLCKOW WAS closely involved with the industrial history of the town and it is fitting that his statue was placed here in Exchange Place, close to the iconic Exchange Building – shown here in around 1908, with Wilson Street on the left and Marton Road on the right. The Exchange Building, which opened on 28 July 1868, contained a large room over 50m long with a vaulted roof, where

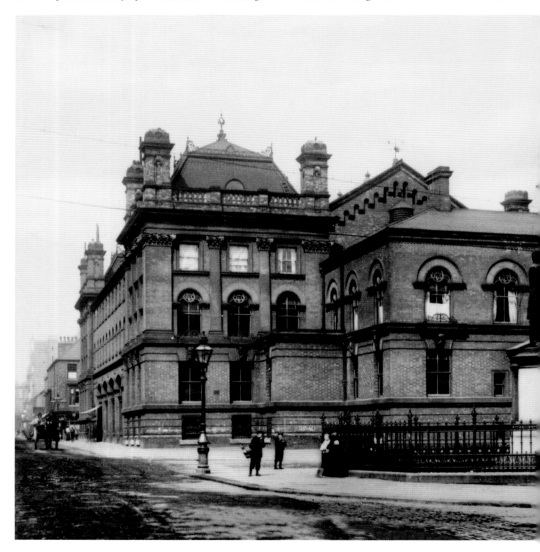

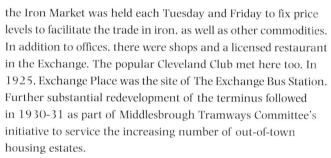

the Iron Market was held each Tuesday and Friday to fix price levels to facilitate the trade in iron, as well as other commodities. In addition to offices, there were shops and a licensed restaurant in the Exchange. The popular Cleveland Club met here too. In 1925, Exchange Place was the site of The Exchange Bus Station. Further substantial redevelopment of the terminus followed in 1930-31 as part of Middlesbrough Tramways Committee's initiative to service the increasing number of out-of-town housing estates.

THE ROUTING OF the A66 Trans-Pennine road through the middle of Exchange Place in the 1980s completely changed the area, slicing Exchange Place in half. The 1931 Exchange Bus Station was demolished along with the Exchange itself; today all that is visible from Wilson Street is one of the supporting walls of the road bridge as it crosses Albert Road. The decision to construct this route was highly controversial, the demolition of the Exchange Building being considered by many to be an act of vandalism, a loss forever of an important part of the history of the town. The road is an important part of Middlesbrough's transport infrastructure, but at what cost?

17

MARTON ROAD

THIS VIEW FROM around 1912 looks across Exchange Place towards Marton Road. A group of boys sit on the octagonal fence encircling the statue of ironmaster Henry Bolckow, who, along with John Vaughan, played an important role in the history of Middlesbrough. Lord Cavendish, watched by what the *Daily Gazette* described as a 'solid mass of humanity', unveiled the statue on 6 October 1881, a major event in the town's fiftieth Jubilee celebrations. Also in view is the Freemason's Hall, which opened on 12 January 1861. The site for the hall cost £159, and the building and furniture cost £838. Partly visible on the left are the impressive Post Office Chambers. Until Middlesbrough got its own post office in the 1840s, letters were brought from Stockton to the town in the Tees Coal Company's letter bag, where they were displayed

in their office window for claiming. Later, postal facilities were based in North Street and Dacre Street and then less commodious premises on Marton Road, before moving on 17 September 1879 to this nearby site, under the management of John Jordison.

ONE OF THE more pleasing trends in the redevelopment of Middlesbrough is the cleaning and restoration of some original buildings. This is particularly evident in the buildings in Exchange Place. Despite its proximity to the A66 (the supporting wall of the road is just visible), Exchange Square (as it is now named) is an elegant tree-lined area once again under the scrutiny of Henry Bolckow, whose statue stands in its midst. Teesside Archives now occupy the distant building in the square. Many people visiting the archives must surely prefer the relative peace and serenity found here today to the noise and bustle of the former bus station.

THE FIRST ELECTRIC TRAM

IN 1897, A Parliamentary Bill sanctioned the building of an electrified tram system from North Ormesby to Norton Green. The laying of the new tracks signified the end of the horse-drawn services, and the last horse-tram from the Exchange to Newport ran on 13 December 1897, and to Linthorpe a week later. The new tram service began operating on 16 July 1898, bringing one of the most up-to-date systems of the time to the town. This image shows some of the crowds who turned out on the first day, here watching the No. 27 and No. 28 trams as they travel along Newport Road close to the Cleveland Hall, the site of today's bus station. The United Presbyterian Church, which stood on the corner of Hill Street, is visible on the left.

Built in 1865, the final service in the church was held on 27 July 1919. It then became the Scala Cinema, eventually closing on 8 April 1961.

TODAY, THE FRONTAGE of the buildings in the immediate foreground (beyond the Princess Alice public house) survive, along with some of the buildings further away, including the old Scala Cinema. However, there has been a major redevelopment of the area and the land around it. On the mid-left can be seen one of the entrances to the Hill Street Shopping Centre; many streets of terraced houses were demolished during the construction of this site. With a similar development opposite – when the bus terminus was rebuilt – many other properties were demolished, giving this area a very different visual profile today.

NEWPORT ROAD AND ST PAUL'S CHURCH

FOR MANY YEARS the only road between Middlesbrough and Stockton was the circuitous route through Linthorpe and Acklam. In 1858, a turnpike was opened across marshland and the old River Tees to Newport village. It went no further until Newport Road was built to Boundary Road across North Acklam, on farmland owned by the Hustler family. One of the main routes into the town, Newport Road, was a busy retail centre with a variety of shops

and products. One shop, Wedgwood's Provisions, which stood on the corner of Unthank Street, can be seen here in around 1910. The spire of St Paul's Church is visible and a tram travels towards the entrance to Parliament Street in the foreground. St Paul's Church was consecrated in 1871, after the Hustler family made a substantial donation towards its construction.

TODAY, NEWPORT ROAD is a shadow of its former self; virtually no original buildings survive along the road itself, although there are some in the immediate area to the east around Parliament Road and Union Street. St Paul's Church survived bombing raids during the Second World War but had become increasingly fragile during the 1960s, and was demolished in 1967. One bit of history to survive is the site of the old Pavilion Theatre on the right, close to the corner of Lamport Street; the name is still visible on the exterior of the building.

CANNON STREET

BUILT IN THE later nineteenth century on land adjacent to the Ironmasters District, Cannon Street has assumed an extraordinary status in the social history of old Middlesbrough. Cannon Street was an area of dense housing and ran parallel to Newport Road, almost a 'community within a community'. There are many tales about life there and Cannon Street is still strongly identified in many people's minds with life in the tight-knit communities of old Middlesbrough. This evocative image from the early 1960s looks from the corner of Duncombe Street towards Boundary Street in the distance (today this is the site of Sainsbury's). In the foreground, Millbank Street crosses Cannon Street, one of many streets to do so as they linked with Newport Road. Many children would have walked this route to reach Marsh Road School, on the left at the end of Millbank Street. Cars and television aerials,

evidence of the modern era, contrast dramatically with the nineteenth-century terraced housing and streets still lit by Victorian gas lamps.

THE CANNON STREET area has suffered at the hands of the developers, with nothing left of what was a substantial area of housing, and, of course, a community of thousands of people. Although the contemporary view was taken close to the location of the old image, only the distant Transporter Bridge and the 'Cannon Park Way' street sign gives any clue that it is the same location. Cannon Street, like much of old Middlesbrough, is gone but not forgotten – there was even a former residents' association in existence in recent times, a fond reminder of the links that still exist for many people.

OLD TOWN HALL AND ST HILDA'S CHURCH

THIS IMAGE SHOWS two icons of the original town, the old Town Hall and St Hilda's Church. While the former still stands, St Hilda's Church was demolished in 1969 – a loss felt keenly by many of the town's residents. The church was built on land donated by the Owners of the Middlesbrough Estate (OME) close to the Market Square. The influence of the OME, keen to have the calming influence of religion in the town, helped to raise a large amount of money from public subscriptions to meet construction costs, and the church was consecrated on 25 September 1840. However, the surrounding burial ground closed in 1854, with burials being transferred to Ayresome Gardens. In 1841, the OME formally handed development of the town over to twelve 'Improvement Commissioners'. In 1846, they erected a Town Hall in the centre of the Market

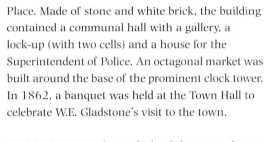

Place. Made of stone and white brick, the building contained a communal hall with a gallery, a lock-up (with two cells) and a house for the Superintendent of Police. An octagonal market was built around the base of the prominent clock tower. In 1862, a banquet was held at the Town Hall to celebrate W.E. Gladstone's visit to the town.

IT IS REGRETFUL that so little of the original town remains less than two centuries after it was first constructed. Today the area is once again open land – if it weren't for the Old Town Hall building it would be almost impossible to locate this scene. This historic Grade II listed building today stands empty and in some state of decay. In recent years it was used as a community centre; now large swathes of grass cover much of the site of the surrounding old town, an ironic reminder that this was, until two centuries ago, open farmland. Various problems have hindered attempts to redevelop the area – neglect and vandalism were major factors in the eventual demolition of St Hilda's.

MIDDLESBROUGH
MARKET PLACE

AT THE CENTRE of the original town was Market Square; home to Middlesbrough Market for more than a hundred years despite attempts to move it elsewhere, especially after the town spilled across the railway line. In 1883, a petition signed by over 2,000 people asked for it to be moved close to Newport Road, while in the late 1930s there were calls to move it close to Grange Road. The opening of the market on 12 December 1840 was marked by a large dinner. The market proved so popular that it was expanded in 1856, followed by a vegetable market, which opened on the corner of East Street in 1861, and which is visible behind the unusual bell tower. A butchers' market opened on the corner of West Street in 1865. Beyond the Town Hall and Market Hall, North Street slopes down to the river. A number of market stalls are shown:

many traders became familiar names in the town, including Walter Bishop, Richardson's, J.D. Lane, Whitfield's, Garbutt's, Bella Miller, and Hartley's. As well as offering a wide variety of locally grown food, there were many amusements to keep people entertained, such as shooting galleries, roundabouts and street entertainers, including Sequah the famous medicine man. The market was so popular it often remained open until midnight.

ALTHOUGH THIS ISN'T an unpleasant scene, it is remarkable to think that this is the site of the busy Market Square seen in the old image. Following the slum clearances of the mid-twentieth century, there were hopes that the town's subsequent redevelopment would revive the strong community it had once been. But the shortcomings of the redevelopment scheme and the relatively brief lifespan of many of the 1960s buildings meant that they became inadequate in less than two decades. There are various reasons why this area has failed to be developed in the way that other Victorian ports have been, such as Liverpool or Hartlepool; the recent renovation of the nearby Customs House has signified some recognition of the town's history – it is to be hoped that there will be more.

ST HILDA'S PLACE

THE LIVING CONDITIONS of some of the inhabitants in the original town left a lot to be desired, as shown by these images of back-to-back housing in the old town. As the population exceeded all original expectations Richard Otley's town plan proved inadequate, with dense house building and infilling on a massive scale choking the precise grid pattern of streets. Dark, gloomy courtyards and small houses without adequate ventilation, sewerage arrangements or even a basic water supply were built, resulting in the slum housing shown here. In many yards families were served by only one communal pump. With much of the old town built on land that was originally low-lying marshes, there were many problems in drainage, meaning that sewage was often incapable of being drained from the basement rooms in particular. Despite a series of cholera and typhoid epidemics hitting the town and several official reports by government inspectors, including the well-known Ranger Report of 1855, little progress was made in addressing these problems. The lack of fresh water was a huge problem – the mains were laid to the area but there was reluctance to accept responsibility for the connection to individual properties. After more virulent epidemics in the 1890s, a government inspector concluded that they were due to the town's 3,000 privy middens being in close proximity to people's homes. The deficiencies in the sewerage system meant that raw sewage was regularly found on some streets. Even when the Corporation voluntarily adopted legislation in 1901, which would have allowed them to address this problem by demolishing the worst slums, they were slow to act and it was not until 1914, after initial pressure from Marion Coates Hansen of the Independent Labour Party, that a report was drawn up outlining solutions to the problem. Inevitably, the onset of the First World War delayed any further action until after the conflict was over. Although a new, compulsory Housing and Town Planning Act required the Corporation to survey the housing needs of the town in 1919, it was to be a further eight years before widespread demolition of Middlesbrough's slum areas began with the Dacre Street Improvement Scheme. By November 1927, the first fifty-seven houses had been cleared and scenes like these were to become a distant memory.

THE CONTEMPORARY PHOTOGRAPH was taken close to where the old Market Square once stood – traces of one of the old streets is still visible in the foreground. It is ironic that there is so much green, sunshine and light where once there would have been decrepit, unlit yards where sunshine and light would have been a rare experience. The sheer openness of the scene is a world away from the smoky, claustrophobic atmosphere that existed in the old yards.

SOUTH STREET

SOUTH STREET WAS a busy southern exit from the town, ideal for the retail trade. This busy scene from around 1908 shows some of the many shops, as well as the overflow of stalls from the market place. The Market Hall is also visible, while the 'Foreign Money Exchange' building on the corner of Henry Street reminds us of the town's former role as a port. Suffield Street, beyond the Exchange, had two public houses, The Fleece and The Globe, on each corner. The drapers, Pottages, close to the corner of Garbutt Street, was very popular with shoppers. Some well-known names in the history of Middlesbrough's retail trade, including Amos Hinton, Matthew

Collingwood and Wilson Newbould, began here. Newbould, who came to the town in 1864, died on 15 May 1896 at the age of only fifty-seven – just a week after the death of his nineteen-year-old son – and they were buried together.

TODAY THE HUSTLE and bustle of this once busy urban scene is but a memory and, although the remains of the road are visible, the area is covered with grass. Attempts at redevelopment have met with mixed results; after the clearances of the late 1950s, many new properties were built. Sadly, by the 1980s these properties too had become slums and many were demolished, to be followed by another rebuilding programme, which it was hoped would bring people into the area. This wasn't a success, however, and these too have been demolished in recent years. Following an announcement from the Mayor in July 2004, St Hilda's was identified as an area for intervention within Middlesbrough. Recently, phase three of the Greater Middlehaven Strategic Framework Plan has included the erection of several new buildings, including the relocated Police Headquarters.

QUEENS SQUARE

THE TOWN QUICKLY expanded southwards as the Owners of the Middlesbrough Estate (OME) sold off various pieces of land. Developers laid down new streets, including the architecturally pleasing area around Queens Square, shown here in around 1903. Wealthy individuals lived here at the Cleveland Buildings including Henry Bolckow from 1841 to 1854 and John Vaughan from 1841 to 1858. To the rear were well laid out gardens looking onto the nearby hills. Opposite, a large, elegant, two-storey redbrick house was owned by local shipbuilder John

Gilbert Holmes, whose sloping lawns reached almost as far as Albert Bridge. Bought by the National Provincial Bank in 1864 as business premises, it was demolished in 1872, when the current building was erected. On the left is Queens Terrace, a stylish terrace of eight houses built in 1850, which today are commercial premises.

IT IS GOOD to see that many of the Grade II listed buildings in Queens Square remain; apart from the modern structure in the right foreground most of the original buildings are easily recognised today, including the mid-nineteenth-century houses once occupied by Bolckow and Vaughan. A blue plaque on the front of the property marks their occupation of the houses. Despite the old cobbles in Queens Square being replaced by tarmac, much of the elegance of the area still remains.

THE NEW
RAILWAY STATION

THE MAJESTIC – A horse-drawn carriage using the branch line – provided a daily service to Stockton until it was replaced in 1834 by a locomotive-drawn service provided by the Stockton & Darlington Railway Company. Three times daily the loco left the town's first station, a wooden hut situated near the original coal staithes. A more substantial building in Commercial Street, opposite the Exchange Hotel, replaced the hut until a new station at the end of Sussex Street opened in 1847, serving the new line to Redcar. The location of the new station caused unrest – a petition protested that the site was too far from the town. A new station was opened on

the same site in 1877, by which time the town had spread beyond the location. The building had a 300-yard arch with a glass roof, which was later destroyed when the station was bombed by enemy aircraft on 3 August 1942. This view shows a busy crowd on the corner of Zetland Road in 1904.

THE MOST OBVIOUS change is the loss of the glass roof, but a careful comparison of the two images reveals several features which have remained unchanged. The basic roofline of the station buildings is similar and, while crowds no longer descend on Zetland Road (today it is a much less used access road to the station), the modern scene does still retain some of the few remaining buildings that date back to a time when Middlesbrough enjoyed prominence as an industrial town.

THE ROYAL EXCHANGE

TO MEET THE needs of the town's
growth as an industrial centre, the
Middlesbrough Exchange Company Ltd
(formed in 1864) inspired the building of
the Exchange. This impressive building
reflected the commercial importance of
the iron industry to the town, as well as
to the regional and national economy.
Opening on 28 July 1868, construction
cost £28,000 despite a 130ft tower being
omitted due to lack of money. The image
clearly shows the fine stone carvings that
adorned the red brick building. Seen from
the junction of Wilson Street and Albert
Road in about 1896, the Exchange, with
its close location to the railway station
making it very accessible for businessmen
visiting the town, had now become the
commercial centre for the iron trade.
The statue of ironmaster John Vaughan

in the distance – unveiled by Sir J.W. Pease on 29 September 1884 as a fitting tribute to this leading figure in Middlesbrough's industrial history – was moved to Victoria Square on 23 October 1914.

THIS MODERN VIEW of the site where the Exchange once stood is taken from the corner of Zetland Street and Albert Road, slightly north of the location of the previous photograph. A classic archway entrance to The Exchange public house stands underneath the A66, the major Trans-Pennine route that thunders with the noise of traffic throughout the day. It is impossible to think what those behind the move to construct the Royal Exchange building would have thought at this contemporary scene – perhaps being men of business, they may have applauded the engineering aspect of this structure, but they surely would have mourned the loss of the Victorian magnificence that was the Royal Exchange.

THE NEW TOWN HALL

FOLLOWING THE VISIT of Prince Arthur, it was over thirty years before the next royal visit to the town, when the Prince and Princess of Wales opened the new Town Hall (or the New Municipal Buildings as they were then called) on 23 January 1889. This was a huge event for Middlesbrough and thousands of people turned out to see the royal visitors. As the Royal train arrived at Middlesbrough railway station at 12.10 p.m., the 1st North York Artillery Volunteers fired a salute from Albert Park; the lengthy royal procession then made its way through streets decorated with flags and other regalia to the Market Square. The *Northern Echo* reported that such was the enthusiasm of the crowds in the old town that at one point the horses in the procession almost went out of control. Brass bands played the National Anthem on every street corner as the procession moved along Linthorpe Road and Grange Road into Upper Albert Road, where 'God Save The Queen' was sung by thousands of children accommodated

in a huge grandstand. Following the official opening, the royal party were treated to a banquet before they departed by train at 3.40 p.m., an event marked by another salute of guns from Albert Park. The momentous day finished with a huge firework display by Messrs James Pain & Son of London, on rough ground that is now Victoria Square, and a performance of the Messiah at the new Town Hall.

LOOKING ACROSS VICTORIA Square over a hundred years later, it is hard to imagine the huge grandstand that stood here on that momentous day in 1889. Then an area described as 'rough land', it was used as a cattle market, a circus, a cycle track and a skating rink in winter, before Colonel S.A. Sadler opened it on 12 July 1901 as Victoria Square, complete with ornamental garden and bandstand, from where the Coldstream Guards provided music. By 1912, as this image shows, seats had been provided for the 'sole use of old people'. The statue of John Vaughan was moved here from Exchange Place on 23 October 1914, joining the statue of Sir Samuel Sadler, which had been placed here on 21 June 1913. Note that the houses in Russell Street and Dunning Street, visible in the old picture, are no more.

NEWPORT ROAD CORNER

THE KING'S HEAD Hotel, seen here on the left in around 1908, stood at No. 1 Newport Road on the junction with Linthorpe Road. The King's Head opened in 1862 as part of the building of the first section of Newport Road. It was a popular venue for local inhabitants, only closing when John Newhouse bought the site for his new store in 1912. Even a century ago this was a popular shopping area, with crowds of people often spilling across from the pavements on to Linthorpe Road.

REMARKABLY, THE NEO-JACOBEAN style of Collingwood's building has survived intact, complete with its classical features including the curved corner, round turret and Dutch gables. The building's east elevation has been extended in an architectural style identical to the original. No longer a jewellery shop, it is now Miss Selfridge, one of several fashion shops trading from this location in recent years. Opposite, the King's Head Hotel was converted into the building we see today when Newhouse's took possession in 1912. The exterior remains largely unchanged, apart from the addition of a top floor. Note the pedestrianisation of Linthorpe Road and Corporation Road.

WESLEYAN
CHAPEL
('BIG WESLEY')

THE WESLEYAN CHAPEL stood on a site occupied today by British Home Stores. Opening on 20 September 1863, it is still remembered by many local people. Beyond the Wesleyan Chapel is the Athenaeum Building, where the Cleveland Literary and Philosophical Society were based. Local people fondly referred to this chapel as 'Big Wesley', a name that has been passed down through the generations. It was a sad day for many when the last service was held here in March 1954, with the building being demolished soon afterwards.

SINCE THE DEMOLITION of the Wesleyan Chapel the site has been occupied by a retail store, this being incorporated into the Cleveland Centre when it opened almost forty years ago. 'Big Wesley' was a dominant building and well-used throughout its history. The author's grandparents married here in 1925, the wedding service being held at the unusually early time of 8 a.m. Years before, a triumphal arch had been constructed here, stretching from the chapel across Linthorpe Road for the Prince and Princess of Wales to pass under as they travelled to open the new Town Hall in 1889.

THE INFIRMARY HOSPITAL

IN THE EARLY 1860s, 'Long Plantation' – an acre of land adjacent to Newport Road - was donated by the Hustler family, along with a financial contribution towards the £7,865 construction costs, for the purpose of building Middlesbrough Infirmary. The new hospital, which replaced a Cottage Hospital built in 1859, was opened by Henry Bolckow on 5 June 1864. Many of its patients were casualties from the nearby Ironmasters District and the hospital soon won the respect and high regard of the citizens of the town.

THE HOSPITAL REMAINED one of the most familiar sites in Middlesbrough until its closure and subsequent demolition in 2008, an act which caused great anger among Middlesbrough citizens. A petition of over 7,000 signatures and a great deal of local media attention failed to save the building from its eventual fate. Today, the site is a Travel Lodge and Aldi supermarket. Middlesbrough Infirmary may have gone but it is certainly not forgotten.

HUGH BELL SCHOOL

HUGH BELL SCHOOL was on a site facing onto Victoria Square. The original site was purchased on 11 September 1889 for £3,375 from the Owners of the Middlesbrough Estate, and was opened as the Grange Road Schools on 2 May 1892 by Alderman T. Hugh Bell. It was renamed Hugh Bell School on 6 December 1898, marking Hugh Bell's role as Chairman of the Middlesbrough School Board. This view, taken from Albert Road, shows Victoria Square on the left. Note the work being carried out to the tramlines.

TEESSIDE LAW COURTS were built on the site of the school in the 1970s. A very different view is seen today, as even the gardens of Victoria Square have been updated and no longer exist in the form they once did. The name of local industrialist Hugh Bell lives on, as a Former Pupils' Society has existed for many years; a reflection of the affection felt for the school.

MIDDLESBROUGH
HIGH SCHOOL

A GROUP OF local industrialists founded one of the town's leading schools, Middlesbrough High School, which opened for boys at No. 1 Grange Road on 15 October 1870. Initially, twenty-five fee-paying pupils were enrolled, but by 1874 numbers had increased to ninety-three. A school for girls opened on 11 August 1874 at No. 37 Grange Road, aided by a grant from local ironmaster Bernard Samuelsson. When a preparatory school was added in 1876, it became clear that a more

substantial building was needed. A site at the southern end of Albert Road – then occupied by allotments – was offered by J.W. Pease and partners. The new buildings, designed by the gothic-revivalist architect Alfred Waterhouse, opened on 15 January 1877. The clock tower, familiar to generations of schoolchildren, is seen here in 1896.

TODAY, THE SITE is part of the University of Teesside and it is pleasing to see that the view is still recognisable, although somewhat changed. The clock tower and the western section still stand, monuments from the past now dwarfed by the huge modern university edifice only yards away. The original school building, which closed in 1959, was cut in half a decade later, when the eastern section of the school was demolished during development of the Further Education buildings. Buildings around the site have also gone, although the white stone building on the left, for many years part of Constantine College and opened by the Prince of Wales (later Edward VIII) on 2 July 1930, has survived.

CARNEGIE LIBRARY

A GENEROUS DONATION of £15,000 from Andrew Carnegie in January 1908 enabled the
Carnegie Library (as it was originally known) to be built on land donated by Sir Hugh Bell
on Grange Road and by Amos Hinton on Dunning Street. Shown here from the south-west,

shortly after being opened by Alderman Amos Hinton on 8 May 1912, the new building replaced the Free Library that had previously been housed in rooms at the Town Hall on the corner of Russell Street and Albert Road.

ON 8 MAY 2012, the library (renamed Middlesbrough Central Library) celebrated its centenary with a number of events, including a visit by the Mayor. Today, it is pleasing to note that not only does the library remain a popular facility, but it also retains many of the original fittings inside. The contemporary view, taken from the steps of Teesside Law Courts, shows the library and the edge of the Victoria Square development. The library building remains the same, but the surrounding landscape has changed, with all traces of previous buildings having gone.

DORMAN MUSEUM

THE DORMAN MUSEUM was opened on 1 July 1904, on land donated by Sir Arthur Dorman, founder of Dorman Long & Co. Ltd, as a memorial to his son George Dorman, who had died in the Boer War. Sir Arthur Dorman also donated £15,000 for the building costs. The museum is well known to several generations of Middlesbrough inhabitants, particularly the collection of stuffed animals that were donated by Sir Alfred Edward Pease.

THE DORMAN MUSEUM continues to be one of the leading attractions in Middlesbrough today. As can be seen, the outer fabric of the museum building remains broadly the same; inside, however, there have been numerous changes with many of the exhibits having been replaced by a series of modern, vibrant displays which relate to the history of the town and the wider world. The excellent attendance at the recent exhibition on Middlesbrough Football Club was an example of this successful approach. The immediate area around the Dorman Museum remains largely unchanged, with Albert Park still providing a valuable adjacent facility.

ALBERT PARK

MIDDLESBROUGH WAS STILL expanding south when this picture from Albert Park towards Linthorpe Road and the yet-to-be built Kensington Road was taken. In fact, if you look carefully, the hedgerows and distant trees that stood on Old Gate farm can be seen, evidence that even in the early 1900s there was still considerable development taking place. HRH Prince Arthur opened Albert Park – named after the late Prince Consort and built on land donated to the town by Henry Bolckow – on Tuesday, 11 August 1868. This was an important event for the town, an endorsement of its importance. The view looks out from Wellingtonia Walk through the magnificent Park Gates, made by Walker's of York and purchased for donation by Henry

Bolckow at an exhibition in York in 1867. Alderman Thomas Sanderson presented the elegant clock in 1900.

THE ORIGINAL GATES have not survived the passing of time but the present gates, which have been in place since 1982, are a worthy replacement and do not detract from the stylish entrance to the park. The clock has been more fortunate and still stands close to the entrance. Part of the West Lodge can also be seen. Albert Park today is still a wonderful facility; a recent restoration project has ensured that it will continue to serve as a vital leisure facility for many years to come. The fields in the previous image have been replaced by rows of houses, including Kensington Road.

GRAND OPERA HOUSE

ANOTHER POPULAR VENUE to carry on the tradition of entertainment established in the old town during the nineteenth century was the Grand Opera House. Built at a cost of £38,000 on the corner of Southfield Road and Linthorpe Road, previously the site of Swathers Carr, the

Opera House opened on 7 December 1903. Many famous artists appeared here, including Charlie Chaplin in 1912, Fred Karno, Gracie Fields and Jack Buchanan. It closed on 21 June 1930 and reopened on 31 March as the Gaumont Cinema. Beyond the Opera House is Southfield Road, then one of the most desirable roads to live in.

TODAY THERE ARE few signs that the elegant opera house ever existed. The Gaumont Cinema survived until 1963; subsequent development has included the building of the new structure that stands on the site today. Much of Southfield Road has gone too. It is strange to think that when this site was part of Swatters Carr Farm, it was open countryside. On 24 July 1879, the Cleveland Agricultural Society held their annual show here, with over 4,000 people attending on a day of sunshine after several days of very heavy rain.

EMPIRE
THEATRE

THE EMPIRE PALACE of Varieties has a distinctive
history stretching back to the days of the music hall.
Built on a site previously used for circus shows, the
Empire had six private boxes and other seating for more
than a thousand people, and was claimed to be 'one

of the most elegant theatres in the provinces'. Many famous entertainers have appeared at the Empire since it opened on 13 March 1899, including Charlie Chaplin, Stan Laurel, Gracie Fields, George Formby, Will Hay, W.C. Fields, Marie Lloyd, and Morecombe and Wise. In 1937, Sir Harry Lauder, returning to the Empire after an absence of thirty-three years, paid tribute to the 'spirited nature' of the audiences there.

THE EMPIRE THEATRE, as it is now known, is still a popular venue with young people flocking to the disco entertainment provided here. The Empire continues to attract well-known names from the entertainment world, including Pete Tong, Testo, Paul van Dyke, Roger Sanchez, The Darkness, Razorlight, Arctic Monkeys, Kaiser Chiefs, Kasabian and the Scissor Sisters.

ACKLAM IRON WORKS

ACKLAM IRONWORKS, OWNED by Stevenson, Jacques & Co., was situated in the northern area of the Ironmasters' District, next to the Linthorpe Works. These two works were close to the old town of Middlesbrough and across the river from the Bell Brothers Ironworks at Port Clarence. This view of the blast furnaces, from about 1912, shows how large they were when compared with the workers standing in the foreground.

IT IS VIRTUALLY impossible to take a photograph from the exact location of the old picture, as this is now part of the Riverside Industrial Park. This image, taken close by,

does, however, show how the area has changed, with the Transporter Bridge once again acting as a guide to our location. This whole stretch of land close to the River Tees has been transformed, with the physical traces of the industrial past having largely disappeared. The many houses that once comprised the Cannon Street area have gone and today a network of new roads and industrial units exist.

DORMAN LONG

THE 1920s WAS a decade of depression for iron and steel companies. At one point, Dorman Long, the leading industrial company in Teesside, were only operating at thirty per cent capacity. It was decided to reorganise its haphazard collection of plants, created through years of taking over smaller companies, by closing the obsolete and ensuring the modern were utilised to their

strengths. The Britannia Works, seen here in around 1930, had originally been leased from Bernard Samuelson to increase the company's pig-iron capacity. It then became part of Dorman Long's long-term reorganisation process – a move that would prove very successful.

THE RECENT HISTORY of steel making on Teesside first came to a halt in 2011 and, in 2012, returning for what we all hope will be a very long time. The steel industry has been synonymous not only with Middlesbrough but with the whole region for almost two centuries, and to lose this heritage would have been a huge blow to the area as a whole. This modern view of the works at Redcar celebrates steel making in the wider Middlesbrough area.

MIDDLESBROUGH DOCKS

SHIPS TRAVELLED TO the port of Middlesbrough from many different places bringing a variety of different cargoes. This view looks from the dock towards the river. Middlesbrough Dock was built on marshland to the east of the original town as an answer to the problems caused by silting-up at the original coal staithes at Port Darlington. The enclosed dock, which had a constant water level to prevent silting-up, was designed by Sir William Cubitt and was opened on 12 May 1842. Facilities were much improved and included ten coal drops served by a fan of railway lines from the Dock Branch, an extension from the original line to Port Darlington. The increasing size of ships and a need to handle other cargoes (following the decline in the shipment of coal) led to several changes in Middlesbrough Dock. When the dock opened, the enclosed water level was 3.6 hectares, but further extensions in 1869, 1885 and 1898 expanded this to 10.1 hectares and 2,134 metres of quayage. The number of sailing ships using the river fell steadily throughout the nineteenth century. By 1890, only thirty-three per cent of ships cleared on the Tees were sailing ships, a figure that dropped to just fourteen per cent by 1913.

THE CONTEMPORARY VIEW of the now defunct Middlesbrough Dock shows some of the old wooden staithes that were once so busy; the clock tower and the nearby Transporter Bridge are also icons from a previous age. A more recent structure are the elliptical rings of the Temenos sculpture, a gigantic piece of art by sculptor Anish Kapoor and designer Cecil Balmond, part of a of a long-term project to regenerate the area. This piece of modern art, part of Tees Valley Regeneration's Middlehaven project, divided opinion, with several people concerned about the reported £2.7m cost. Whatever your opinion, the 45m-tall mast of the Temenos structure certainly stands out.

FERRY LANDING,
OLD MIDDLESBROUGH

AS WELL AS the railway and the various tram services on offer, people in Middlesbrough also had the use of ferry services. Rival services operated by Mr C.C. Duncan and a Mr Dixon sailed from Newport Landing to Stockton, with an additional service being operated later by Imperial Tramways. The unreliability of the services, as well as the coming of the electrified tram service, eventually reduced passenger numbers and the ferry service was discontinued in 1898. A main ferry service – heavily used by workmen – operated across the river from the quay at Ferry Road, in the old town, to Port Clarence. Two of the best-known boats were the *Hugh Bell*, launched in 1884, and the *Erimus*, launched on 15 September 1888. The *Erimus* was licensed to carry 927 passengers. Both boats operated until the Transporter Bridge opened in 1911, when they were sold to Messrs Pollock, Brown of Southampton – the *Erimus* incidentally being sold for £725.

TODAY, THE VIEW from the old ferry landing, close to the Transporter Bridge, shows a much quieter river. Across the river, the industry that once operated on the northern bank has long since gone, and only the distance steel works offer any clue as to the rich industrial heritage of the area. The flags seen here mark the centenary of the opening of the Transporter Bridge.

TRANSPORTER BRIDGE

THE TRANSPORTER BRIDGE, which celebrated its centenary in October 2011, has become an iconic regional landmark. The Bill for building the bridge received Royal Assent on 4 July 1907, and on 3 August 1910 two foundation stones were laid by the Mayor, Lt-Col T. Gibson-Poole, and Alderman Joseph MacLauchlan, who first instigated the scheme. HRH Prince Arthur of Connaught, KG, who was received as the guest of the Mayor, Sir Hugh Bell, at his country home,

Rounton Grange, opened the bridge, which cost just over £87,000 to build. On the day the bridge was opened, Prince Arthur passed on his journey to Middlesbrough through the toll bar at Grove Hill as his father had done when opening Albert Park in 1868. From there the Prince

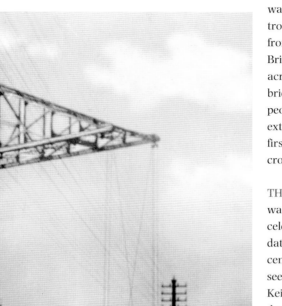

was escorted to the Transporter Bridge by a troop from the Yorkshire Hussars. This image, from around 1921, shows the Transporter Bridge in operation, looking from Port Clarence across to the old town of Middlesbrough. The bridge was an immediate success, with 6,290 people using it on the first day, many paying an extra three pence to walk across the top. In the first year, 2,657,206 people used the bridge to cross the river.

THE CENTENARY OF the Transporter Bridge was commemorated by a number of different celebrations, both before and on the official date, 17 October 2011. One highlight of the centenary was the lighting up of the bridge, as seen in this image taken by local photographer Keith Kirtley. A lot of memories were exchanged during the celebrations and it was fitting that so much attention was given to a structure that has become a symbol of Middlesbrough.

NEWPORT LANDING

THE NEED FOR a bridge linking the town with the rapidly developing industrial area north of the river had been recognised in the early 1920s. Having decided upon a bridge at Newport, the Tees Bridge Act was given Royal Assent on 4 June 1930. Construction began soon after; this view (right) shows the early construction north of the river of a new road built to link the bridge with the nearby ICI complex and village of Billingham. Development is ongoing south of the river, where access to the new bridge meant demolishing several houses in Calvert Street and Samuelson Street, as well as the buildings at Newport Station.

THE CONTEMPORARY VIEW, taken just beyond the Newport Bridge, shows the point where Billingham Beck joins the River Tees. The most remarkable point is the return to nature on both banks after many years of being a site of heavy industry – particularly at Middlesbrough, where Newport Iron Works occupied this site. There are still signs of industry close to the river but it is very different from previous years. The river itself has undergone considerable change and is much less polluted today.

NEWPORT BRIDGE

A TUG PASSES in 1937 under the raised central section of the Newport Bridge, the presence of industry clearly visible with the chimneys of Newport Ironworks belching out industrial grime. Originally built in the second half of the nineteenth century on reclaimed marshland between Newport and the old town, the ironworks were part of an area aptly named the 'Ironmasters' District'. The rapid expansion of the industry, which followed the finding of local iron ore in 1850, meant that by 1871 there were already seven blast furnaces operating at the works, the resultant smoke pouring out over the adjacent area of housing.

ALTHOUGH THE ROAD bridge is now permanently locked down, the bridge is still a unique construction. It is remarkable to see two such individual pieces of iconic engineering as the Newport Bridge and the Transporter Bridge only a short distance from each other. Even more amazing is the successful regeneration that has returned the area beyond the bridge back to green fields. Those who remember this area as a smoky, grimy, industrial site will appreciate just how extensive the change has been. Now wildlife once more lives in these green fields close to the bridge, as it did for hundreds of years when this was isolated farmland.

OLD GATE FARM

ON 17 APRIL 1890, a newspaper advertisement carried details of a forthcoming auction at the Grand Hotel Middlesbrough, where Lot 1 was 'building land and the farmhouse at Old Gate Farm'. This was a time when the town was still expanding south along Linthorpe Road, although there was little development west of Linthorpe Road across to Newport. The ancient hamlets of Ayresome and old Linthorpe still existed; hedgerows and trees lined the old pathways and sailors' trods that criss-crossed the open fields. Looking west from Old Gate Farm was the neighbouring farm, Ayresome Grange, only four fields away. Old Gate Farm, seen here in 1902, was situated close to the site of Ayresome Park, which was built in 1903. It was the home of Middlesbrough Football Club for ninety-two years. Formed in 1876, the club had, by February

1880, moved to a new ground in Linthorpe Road, where they remained for twenty-three years before moving to Ayresome Park. The ground, designed by the doyen of football ground designers, Archibald Leitch, was built on land that was once part of Old Gate Farm.

REMARKABLY, THE WINDOW in the new housing seen behind the farmhouse in the previous image is still visible in this modern image. The house stands on Kensington Road and allows us to have a precise location for the site of the old farm. As always, it is difficult to think that this urban scene was green fields and hedgerows for hundreds of years. When first constructed, these properties were considered to be slightly 'up-market' compared with others closer to the town. This area was still close to the border between town and country and, as such, properties were larger and more spacious. Ironically, Ayresome Park has also become part of the history of the area, having been demolished after the club moved out in 1995.

THE RIVERSIDE STADIUM

IN 1995, MIDDLESBROUGH Football Club made an ambitious and much-publicised move across town to a new stadium built on an industrial site close to the old Middlesbrough Dock. The move was highly debated at the time, with many fans wanting to retain the link with Ayresome Park by redeveloping that site. But the ambition of the club's young Chairman, Steve Gibson, won through and the new stadium was constructed. The building of the new stadium caused much excitement and fans flocked to see the new construction. This view looks towards the distant Transporter Bridge, with the construction of the West Stand visible on the left. A few fans look through the fencing in curiosity – very few people get to see their clubs' stadium being built!

TODAY, THE RIVERSIDE Stadium stands as a tribute to those who brought it about – especially Steve Gibson, who was clearly the driving force at this time. Since Middlesbrough played their first game against Chelsea here in August 1995, they have seen many changes in fortune, but it would be true to say that for many fans those early years were exciting times. The modern picture shows how close to the river the new stadium actually is, with dockside buildings visible in the distance.

THE AVENUE, LINTHORPE

A TRAM APPROACHES the junction of The Crescent and The Avenue, which heads off towards the right. These impressive semi-detached and detached properties were close to New Linthorpe, known locally as 'the village'. At this time, the shops provided an essential service to the new properties in this rapidly growing suburban development. The tram service terminated at The Crescent and then ran back through the town to Ferry Road, an important link to town for residents of Linthorpe.

THE BRICK CHIMNEY on the property located in the right foreground behind the trees helps to align with some precision this modern image with that of a hundred years ago. These houses are still very desirable properties, although Linthorpe village is a less distinct community than it once was. This is still a bus route, but with the increase in the use of motor cars it is a less important service than it once was. On the left, behind the trees, is St Mary's Care Home.

'THE VILLAGE' LINTHORPE

THIS IMAGE SHOWS Linthorpe village in about 1910, with James Henry Ball's Post Office stores open on the corner of Chipchase Road. Local residents referred to this commercial area as 'the village', and it certainly offers a contrast to the housing found further north towards the town. The tram heading towards us terminated at The Crescent, having travelled from Ferry Road in the old town.

THERE IS STILL a post office on Chipchase Road but today it is a short distance away from the one shown in the previous image. The property where it was previously located has been demolished and the site is now occupied by a leisure business. The entrance to Stonehouse Street, visible in the image from 1910, remains today, though many buildings around it have either changed in their purpose or have disappeared altogether.

83

ACKLAM ROAD

ALTHOUGH MIDDLESBROUGH
DEVELOPED within a relatively
short period of time, it was
only after the First World War
that the development began to
reach areas like Acklam. Until
recent times, West Acklam (as it
was then named) was a 'closed
village', part of the Hustler
Estate, with the Hustler family
still living at Acklam Hall.
In this wonderfully evocative
image from 1903, a group of
people pose next to a hedgerow;
in the distance a pony and

trap approach the village smithy, close to the driveway to Acklam Hall. The low-roofed
building in the foreground is today part of the Master Cooper public house; on the left,
just out of view, is the trackway to Acklam vicarage (today this is Church Lane).

THE DEVELOPMENT FROM 1903 is extensive; the quiet country lane is now a busy road
junction with Church Lane on the left and Trimdon Avenue to the right. Swathes of housing
have replaced fields and hedgerows; the gradual development of the 1930s and an expansive
post-war building programme have made Acklam a part of urban Middlesbrough. Remarkably,
the houses in the 1903 image are still visible in this contemporary view, surrounded by
modern development.

MARTON BURN ROAD

AS MANY OF the slum areas in old Middlesbrough were being demolished, new areas of housing were being constructed south of the town. These new residential areas offered much better housing facilities than existed in the town. Houses were more spacious, many had gardens, and the estates were better planned. As can be seen in this image from 1930, there were wide, tree-lined roads – look at the young trees newly planted – and for many people who moved out from the town this was an idyllic existence. There was a frequent bus service to ensure links with town were maintained – this image shows

the 'C' service which ran on a circular route from the Exchange to Grove Hill, then through Linthorpe village and back to town. Middlesbrough uniquely used letters for its bus services rather than numbers.

TODAY THIS IS still a residential area and, although there has been redevelopment in recent years, it is pleasing to see that the trees appear to have survived into maturity. The unique bus services are no longer – most were changed to numbers in the 1970s. The residential area is still an important one, as many of the other housing estates closer to the town were all demolished in the post-1945 era.

NORTH ORMESBY CHURCH

HOLY TRINITY CHURCH in Market Square, North Ormesby, *c.* 1908. Standing on the corner of Charles Street and the Market Place, Holy Trinity Church was consecrated on 26 November 1869. It has had various extensions, including the addition of the tower in 1880 and the clock in 1883. North Ormesby developed after 1860, and, like Middlesbrough, is a purpose-built community. While it has remained in the shadow of Middlesbrough, the people of North Ormesby have always had their own sense of community and identity.

HOLY TRINITY CHURCH still stands today, though most of the immediate area has either been completely demolished or changed beyond recognition. The Market Square was once the hub of the suburb but, today, with so many people having moved away, it is no longer the centre of the community.

NORTH ORMESBY
CROSSING

THIS VIEW FROM around 1908 looks toward North Ormesby level crossing and the junction of Smeaton Street and West Terrace. The old toll bar, which operated until 1916, can also be seen located close to the signal box. The railway, which opened in 1854, originally ran from Middlesbrough to Guisborough and later to Whitby via Battersby Junction. Two carts wait outside the coal depot on the right, while more carts have just passed through the toll bar.

IT IS IMPOSSIBLE today to obtain an image similar to the previous image as the routing of the A66 Trans-Pennine road has obliterated virtually all signs of this part of North Ormesby. The railway to Whitby still operates but there is no sign now of the level crossing nor of Smeaton Street. It is almost as if it was never there at all.

MARTON
ROAD
TOLL BAR

TOLL BARS WERE erected in the
nineteenth century on all privately
owned roads. Although some had
been abolished before 1914, an Act
was passed abolishing the five which
remained in the Middlesbrough area
from 31 July 1916. A commemorative
programme accompanied the formal
ceremony, bringing an end to the toll
bars and allowing open access to
the town.

THE TOLL BAR cottage on Marton
Road still stands nearly a century
later, but is no longer on the perimeter
of the town. Of course, this is now a

busy road into Middlesbrough, but the survival of the cottage is a reminder of a time before the age of modern motoring. It is also an example of how evidence of Middlesbrough's past can still be found even if it is not easy to find. Today, toll bars exist on few roads – the M6 motorway is one example – but a hundred years ago they were a part of daily life.

MARTON HALL

HENRY BOLCKOW AND John Vaughan were key individuals in the development of modern Middlesbrough. Like many Victoran entrepreneurs, their wealth was put into the purchase of fine properties. Both lived in Queens Square before moving out to the south of the town. Vaughan bought Gunnergate Hall whilst Bolckow purchased Marton Estate in 1853. Before moving there in 1856 he had Marton Hall built, a wonderful period example of Victorian architecture. He continued to improve the grandeur of the Hall and its grounds, in which he planted many rare trees. He also amassed a fine art collection, which passed to his nephew Carl but, due to the industrial recession of 1888, it was sold in London on 5 May that year. Its Carrara marble columns and staircase exemplified the elegance of the Hall.

THE DEMOLITION OF buildings in the early 1960s was not confined to the old town. Marton Hall, regarded by many as one of Middlesbrough's most elegant buildings, was demolished in 1960 – an event which even today, fifty-two years later, is still hotly debated by those who believe that it should have been saved. Whatever your view, it is sad to see so much elegance destroyed. The Council had taken the decision to demolish the Hall in 1959, but on 4 June 1960, soon after work began, the building caught fire and a large part of it was destroyed. In 1978, the Captain Cook Museum opened on the site and today, as can be seen in the contemporary photograph, only one fragment of the old building remains. This final picture symbolises the loss of so many buildings in recent years. Much has been lost and, although a more sympathetic attitude in recent years has paid tribute to Middlesbrough's rich heritage, it will always be asked, 'Is it too little, too late?'

If you enjoyed this book, you may also be interested in . . .

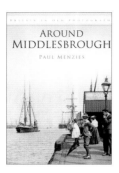

Around Middlesbrough In Old Photographs
PAUL MENZIES

This collection of over 200 archive images traces some of the changes that have taken place in and around Middlesbrough during the last century, as many old agricultural communities were swallowed up by the development of modern industry. With chapters on work, industry, sport and local events, *Around Middlesbrough* offers a rare insight into a vanished way of life and is sure to appeal to everyone with an interest in the history of the town.

978 0 7524 5730 7

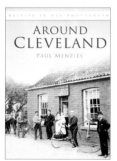

Around Cleveland In Old Photographs
PAUL MENZIES

Richly illustrated and filled with historical insight and local reminiscences, the story of Cleveland and it's surrounding villages is told through detailed chapters on schools, worship, leisure and work. All aspects of everyday life is here, providing a rare insight into a vanished way of life. *Around Cleveland* will appeal to all who know and love this area.

978 0 7524 5136 7

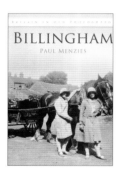

Billingham In Old Photographs
PAUL MENZIES

In 1900, Billingham was a rural community with a history going back over 1,000 years. This collection of archive photographs celebrates more than a century of history: beginning in the very earliest days of photography, it moves from the country lanes and farms of the 1920s to the factories and industries of the 1960s and the bustling town of today. This book will delight everyone who knows the town.

978 0 7524 4838 1

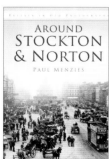

Stockton & Norton In Old Photographs
PAUL MENZIES

This selection of 200 photographs provides a nostalgic insight into the changing face of the neighbouring communities of Stockton and Norton-on-Tees over the last century. Each image is accompanied by a detailed caption, bringing the past to life and describing many aspects of life in the area, including chapters on work, industry and transport, as well as providing a vital record of vanished vistas and past practices.

978 0 7524 5731 4

Visit our website and discover thousands of other History Press books.

www.thehistorypress.co.uk